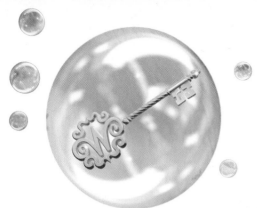

Program Authors

Diane August

Donald R. Bear

Janice A. Dole

Jana Echevarria

Douglas Fisher

David Francis

Vicki Gibson

Jan Hasbrouck

Margaret Kilgo

Jay McTighe

Scott G. Paris

Timothy Shanahan

Josefina V. Tinajero

McGraw Hill Education

Cover and Title pages: Nathan Love

www.mheonline.com/readingwonders

Send all inquiries to:
McGraw-Hill Education
2 Penn Plaza
New York, NY 10121

ISBN: 978-0-07-679344-0
MHID: 0-07-679344-3

Printed in the United States of America.

2 3 4 5 6 7 8 9 RMN 20 19 18 17 16

A

Unit 2 Let's Explore

The Big Idea: What can you find out when you explore?

Week 1 · Tools We Use 4

Phonics: *Pp* 6
Words to Know: *a* 7
Pam Can See Fiction 8
We Can See! Nonfiction 14
Writing and Grammar: Informative Text 20

Week 2 · Shapes All Around Us . . . 22

Phonics: *Tt* 24
Words to Know: *like* 25
We Like Tam! Fiction 26
I Like Sam Fiction 32
Writing and Grammar: Informative Text 38

Week 3 · World of Bugs 40

Phonics: Review *m, a, s, p, t* 42
Words to Know: *the, we, see, a, like* 43
Pat Fiction 44
Tap! Tap! Tap! Nonfiction 50
Writing and Grammar: Informative Text 56

Essential Question

How do tools help us to explore?

Go Digital!

(frame)Dmitriy Sechin/Alamy

COLLABORATE

Talk About It

What tool is the girl using?

4

Come and Explore!

Say the name of each picture.

Read the words.

 Pam   **map**   **sap**

a

I look at **a** map.

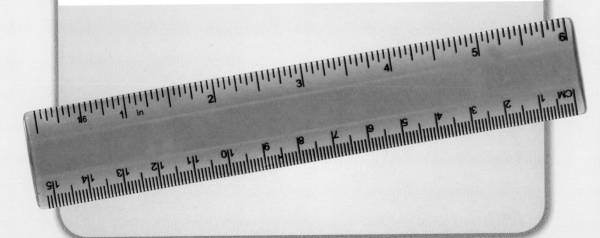

Pam can use **a** ruler.

Pam Can See

Pam can see a .
pot

9

Pam can see a .

pen

Pam can see a .

pad

Pam can see a .

pillow

12

Pam can see Sam!

We Can See!

14

We can see **a** map.

We can see a .

parrot

We can see a .

seal

17

We can see a .

panda

Can the see the ?

panda parrot

Write About the Text

Pam Can See

Pages 8–13

Logan

I answered the question: **How is the register a handy tool for Sam?**

Student Model: *Informative Text*

This tool helps Sam work.

Clues

I used the picture to understand how the register helps Sam.

It adds Pam's things.

Grammar

The word **adds** is a **verb.**

Details
I used evidence to tell why the register is a handy tool.

It tells Pam what to pay. ←

Your Turn  COLLABORATE

How is the shopping cart a handy tool for Pam and her mother? Include text evidence.

Go Digital!
Write your response online.
Use your editing checklist.

21

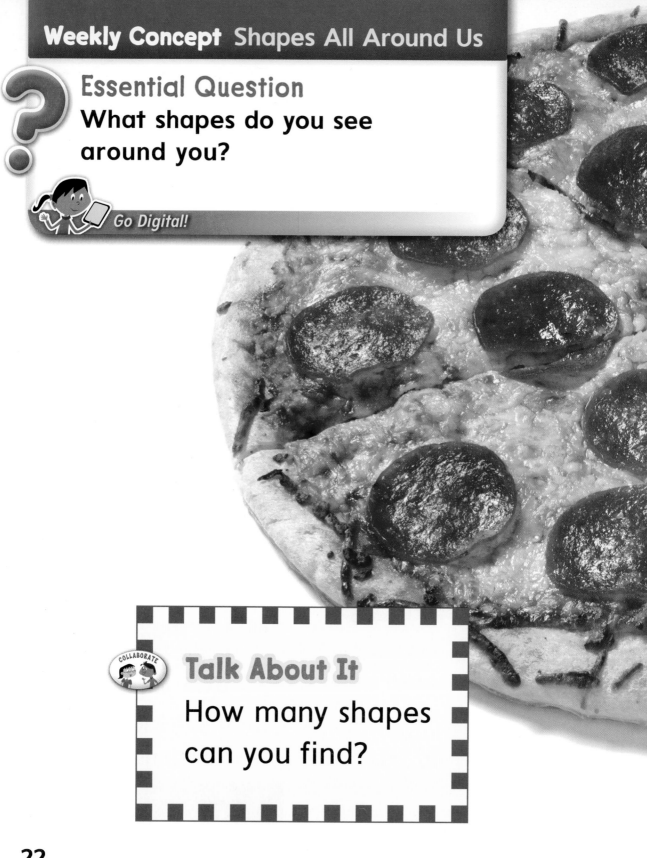

Essential Question

What shapes do you see around you?

Go Digital!

COLLABORATE

Talk About It

How many shapes can you find?

Name That Shape

Say the name of each picture.

Read each word.

at   **mat**   **pat**

tap   **sat**   **Tam**

like

We **like** pizza!

I **like** the tent.

We Like Tam!

Tam can see Pam.

Tam can see Sam.

Sam can tap the .
bell

29

Tam can tap, tap the .

bell

We **like** Tam!

Virginia Allyn

I Like Sam

Jennifer Bell

Sam can pat the cap.

Jennifer Bell

33

34

Sam can pat the .

ball

Sam can tap the .

drum

35

Sam can tap the .

nut

36

I **like** Sam!

Jennifer Bell

Pages 26–31

Write About the Text

Maria

I answered the question: **How is Tam taken care of by the class?**

Student Model: *Informative Text*

They give Tam a home.

Clues

I saw in the picture that Tam has a special home.

38

Details
I told about how Pam cares for Tam.

Pam pats Tam.

The class loves Tam.

Your Turn

COLLABORATE

Look at pages 28 to 30. How does Tam feel about Sam? Include text evidence.

Go Digital!
Write your response online.
Use your editing checklist.

Essential Question

What kinds of bugs do you know about?

Go Digital!

Bugs, Bugs, Bugs

 Talk About It

What do you know
about this bug?

Review Letter Sounds

Say the name of each picture.

Read each word.

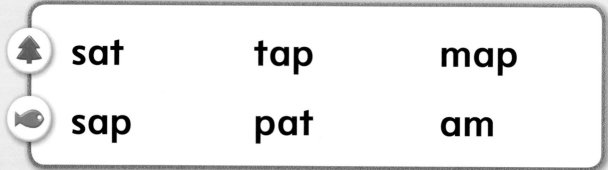

Read Together

Review Words

Read the words and sentences.

🍎 **the**   **we**   **see**

⭐ **a**   **like**

🌲 **We** can **see** **a** spider web.

🐟 Sam and I **like** **the** ant.

Pat

I am Pat.

I am at **the** .

rock

I can **see** **a**  .
bug

47

I tap the 🌾 plant.

I **like** the  .

bug

49

Tap! Tap! Tap!

I am at **the** .

lake

I can **see** the 🐜 .

ant

I can see a .

bee

I **like** to see the 🐞!

bug

We see it tap, tap, tap!

Write About the Text

Pages 44–49

✗ Yasmin

I answered the question: **Why do you think Pat tapped the plant?**

Student Model: *Informative Text*

Pat wants the bug.

It is on the plant.

Pat taps to get the bug.

Clues

I used the picture to figure out why Pat taps the plant.

Grammar

The word **taps** is a **verb.**

Your Turn

Where does Pat live? How do you know?

Go Digital!
Write your response online.
Use your editing checklist.